eXtreme ANIMALS

eXtreme ANIMALS

Sarah Creese

make
believe
ideas

Extreme animals soar in the sky,
build large webs, and go racing by.
They are friendly or scary and
they might make you scream—
but don't forget that all of them
are totally extreme!

Reading together

This book is an ideal first reader for your child, combining simple words and sentences with stunning color photography of real-life animals. Here are some of the many ways you can help your child take those first steps in reading.
Encourage your child to:

- Look at and explore the detail in the pictures.

- Sound out the letters in each word.

- Read and repeat each short sentence.

Look at the pictures

Make the most of each page by talking about the pictures and finding key words. Here are some questions you can use to discuss each page as you go along:

- Why do you like this animal?

- What would it feel like to touch?

- What makes it extreme?

- Does it look cute or scary?

Sound out the words

Encourage your child to sound out the letters in any words he or she does not know. Look at the common "key" words listed at the back of the book and see which of them your child can find on each page.

Test understanding

It is one thing to understand the meaning of individual words, but you need to make sure that your child understands the facts in the text.

- Play "find the obvious mistake." Read the text as your child looks at the words with you, but make an obvious mistake to see if he or she catches it. Ask your child to correct you and provide the right word.

- After reading the facts, close the book and think up questions to ask your child.

- Ask your child whether a fact is true or false.

- Provide your child with three answers to a question and ask him or her to pick the correct one.

Quiz pages

At the end of the book there is a simple quiz. Ask the questions and see if your child can remember the right answers from the text. If not, encourage him or her to look up the answers.

Extreme animals

Who is the tallest, the fastest, the largest, and the oldest? Let's explore the world of extreme animals!

Giraffes are the TALLEST animals! They live in Africa and can reach tasty treetop leaves using their long necks.

Giraffes can be almost 20 feet (6 meters) tall.

African elephants are the LARGEST animals on land.

African elephants weigh up to 27,000 pounds (12.25 tons).

They can spend
almost a whole
day eating!

ear

trunk

toenails

tusk

The cheetah is a speedy sprinter! It is the FASTEST RUNNING animal. It also has very good eyesight, which helps it to hunt in the day.

Cheetahs can run at over 62 mph (100 kph).

Parakeets are the
MOST TALKATIVE birds!
In the wild, they can be
found in Australia.

One parakeet learned how
to say over 1,700
different words.

The Galapagos giant tortoise
holds the record for the
OLDEST animal
living on land.

The oldest Galapagos giant tortoise lived for 176 years!

The whale shark is the LARGEST FISH in the sea! It can grow to be as long as a school bus!

The longest whale sharks are over 40 feet (12 meters) long.

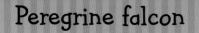

The peregrine falcon is the FASTEST animal! It dives through the air at high speeds to catch its prey.

Peregrine falcons can dive at about 145 mph (230 kph).

Whoosh!

Golden orb-weavers are the spiders that build the LARGEST and STRONGEST WEBS using their silk.

The largest webs can measure over 3 feet (1 meter) from edge to edge.

Tigers are the LARGEST CATS in the world. Their striped fur helps them to hide when they are hunting.

Siberian tigers are the largest of all the tigers. They can weigh over 675 pounds (300 kilograms).

paw

teeth

fur

eye

25

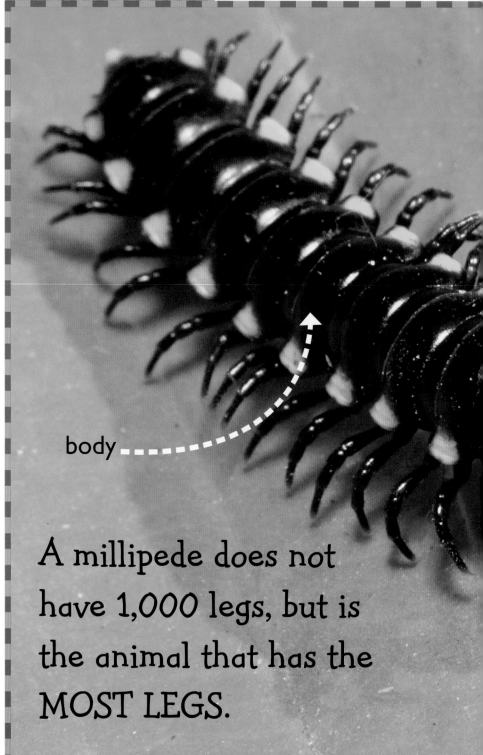

body

A millipede does not
have 1,000 legs, but is
the animal that has the
MOST LEGS.

A millipede with 750 legs holds the record for the greatest number of legs!

leg

head

antenna

What do

1. Which is the largest animal on land?

The African elephant.

2. Which big cat has striped fur?

The tiger has striped fur.

3. Where do giraffes live?

Giraffes live in Africa.

you know?

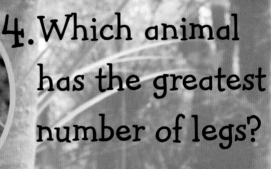

4. Which animal has the greatest number of legs?

The millipede.

5. Which is the largest fish in the sea?

The whale shark.

6. How old was the oldest Galapagos giant tortoise?

The oldest Galapagos giant tortoise was 176 years old.

Dictionary

sprinter
A sprinter runs very fast over short distances.

treetop
The top part of a tree is called the treetop.

talkative
A talkative person is someone who likes to talk a lot!

silk
Silk is made by spiders and other animals. It is very strong and soft.

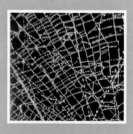

tusk
A tusk is a long, pointed tooth. Elephants have tusks.

I • up • look • we • like • and • on • at • for

a • he • is • go • you • are • this • going • they • away • play • put • all

day • get • come • in • have • ot • me • she • see • it • yes • can • am

Key words

Here are some key words used in context.
Make simple sentences for the other
words in the border.

I live **the** longest.

I **can** run fast.

I build **big** webs.

I can eat **all** day.

I **am** the tallest animal.

the • was • big • my • went • no • to • were •